CELEBRATE YOU!

Self-Healing Through Art And Affirmations

Faridi McFree

A DOLPHIN BOOK
Doubleday & Company, Inc.
Garden City, New York
1982

Dolphin Books/Doubleday/1982

ISBN: 0-385-17730-5

Library of Congress Catalog Card Number: 81-43120

First edition

Dedication

To my Mom, who was the most sensitive and tender, loving and unselfish person I have ever known. Thank you, my Dear Mother, for teaching me love, trust, and honesty. Without these qualities, I would never have been able to share my life with others through my art. Without these qualities, I would never have been able to believe in myself.

My Mom died a few years ago because she did not believe in herself. She died because she accepted sour belief systems about herself.

She died an alcoholic.

I would never have believed in my art or created this book . . . without you . . .

Acknowledgments

To all my new age friends who, since 1973, shared and experienced my *sweat and tears* to "help raise the consciousness of the planet" for more love, peace and harmony . . . through the healing arts . . .

Especially . . .

MICKEY McFREE — my former husband and mentor. During our sixteen-year marriage, he encouraged me and shared with me his love and devoted strength. Without his brilliant, creative mind, I would never have been opened to the possibility of developing as an artist. Thank you, Mickey dear . . . Forever . . . "Me" . . .

My father and immediate family, especially my magnificent niece, MARILYN BENNETT; ED JUSTIN, CLIFF LOEB, SHERRY ROBB & FAMILY, MARK HOWARD, HAROLD WARSHAY, MARIE DUTTON BROWN, LOUISE & THOM HARTMAN, MYRNA & BOB YOUDELMAN, ED KHOURI & FAMILY, FRANK PERRELLA, FLORENCE HORN, JOYCE SIMON, MARCIA STONE, DR. RUSSELL DESMARIS & FAMILY, BARBARA MARTIN, FRED PAGNANI . . . your love of my art, coupled with your worldly counsel, financial and moral support, will be remembered . . . always . . .

With MICHAEL ANTHONY RIDDELL I share the Unconditional Love of Being soulmates, helpmates, co-workers and friends of St. Francis & St. Clare and the Spirit of the Child in living daily Hope and Faith here upon Mother Earth ... "Rainbow of Love".

Love-In-Action ... LINDY HESS, LAURA VAN WORMER, RALLOU M. HAMSHAW, CY ROGERS, JAMES E. BARRY, DEBBIE PARNON ...

BEATTY RUTMAN — special thanks to a woman of great strength and role model for any mother or grandmother! I love you for the influence you have had in my life ... as an artist ...

And ... my deepest appreciation to the man I love for his continued inspiration. B'HABECK ... the melody lingers ...

Introduction

Picasso once said, "The day will come when the sight of a painting will ease the pain of a toothache." Picasso was speaking in parables, perhaps thinking of the effect a combination of colors might produce on a man who knows how to contemplate or has learned to see "WITH HIS WHOLE SOUL," that is to say, with nothing interfering with the trajectory of his gaze . . .

Well . . . that day has come . . . my art and affirmations are healing . . .

Since 1973, I have pioneered self-healing through art and affirmations and have witnessed miracles right before my eyes. I was shocked and surprised when I began to document the creative and therapeutic affect of the art on people. Many people from various life-styles have experienced incredible responses!

* * *

An architect who was unable to close a deal he was negotiating realized how little confidence he had in himself. Through the art and affirmations, he closed a deal for two million dollars. The art reaffirmed confidence in his innate abilities.

A lawyer experienced negative frustrating thoughts that were immobilizing him and seriously affecting his law practice. The affirmation "I am young, vital, and strong," repeated every morning and evening, enabled him to reduce stress and strain.

A woman who was feeling that her husband was not paying enough attention to her looked at the art and thought about the affirmation "I AM TOO BUSY TO BE JEALOUS." She proclaimed, "My jealousy is the problem. I am creating a negative situation in my marriage."

Another woman, who spent too many hours depressed about aging, was inspired and became more youthful after she viewed the art. Her daily affirmation is "AS I MATURE, I GET BETTER AND BETTER."

The art has helped many people reinforce their will to live and develop the ability to find meaning in their life. People who could not draw produced artwork; children of divorced parents exhibited more confidence and more creativity, resulting in scholastic achievement. Abused children became more confident and creative, demonstrating a definite need for this reinforcement. Equally remarkable responses have resulted from my work with drug abusers, alcoholics, mentally disturbed and physically ill people.

A woman wrote after viewing and using the art and affirmations, "At first a great many negative feelings surfaced. However, I felt strong and confident enough to face them and get them out of my life. Then little by little, I began to feel better about my-self. The past few months, I had a number of family tragedies and I truly feel that because of the art and affirmations, I was better equipped to handle them. Secondly, your art, along with the affirmations, acted as a powerful catalyst for me artistically. I became absolutely prolific. I wrote three movie outlines, a TV pilot, and an article for a national newspaper. Be-lieve it or not, I did all this within one month."

Recently, after reading the article "IMAGES THAT HEAL" in *Psychology Today* magazine, tears came to my eyes . . . tears of joy . . . but at the same time, my heart was deeply saddened when I read of the hardships that Dr. Simonton and his wife, Stephanie, have endured the last few years. The Simontons have been pioneering the concept that negative emotions cause dis-ease. Changing your inner atti-tudes about self can actually cure and heal most dis-eases. They state that if you believe in yourself and think about yourself in a positive manner, you will manifest a life filled with health and happiness. How I identified with them!

Like the Simontons, I have also been scorned. Emotionally, I have suffered tremendous pain for the past three years due to my own personal hardships. However, it was my art, affirmations, and visualizations that kept me alive, well free of dis-ease. THROUGH MY ART AND TECHNIQUES, I WAS ABLE TO RELEASE ALL THE NEGATIVE EMOTIONS OF HELPLESSNESS, HOPELESSNESS, ANGER, DISTRESS, DISAPPOINTMENT, LOSS AND DESPAIR ... ALONG WITH RESENTMENT AND SELF-PITY. It wasn't easy but I did it! The article "Images That Heal" reinforced my belief that my intuitional self was POSITIVE rather than NEGATIVE ... THE ART SAVED MY LIFE!

This realization of self-awareness is essential to our everyday existence. When we are aware of our feelings and the way we receive reactions from others, we can lead such free and beautiful lives. Emotions like jealousy, envy, anger, and depression can only lead to self-destruction and unhealthy relationships.

How "we create our own reality" is a simple concept. Yet, we all need to be reminded that we do receive what we give out. We scream at our children with impatience and we get back frustration. We walk around with our heads down feeling old and useless, and people perceive our lack of energy and don't want to be around us.

Art and affirmations are not cure-alls. But used positively and consistently, they do enable us to remember that we have the *power* to create for ourselves a more positive and beautiful outlook for ourselves and others.

John Lennon, one of our greatest contemporary artists, in a statement shortly before his death said, "No one can cure you ... you cure you ... take responsibility for yourself and have faith in yourself."

Please ... set aside your negative expectations and tune into your natural self ... the beauty and divinity that already exist ... Godhood of self and others. Tune into a reality where there is no sickness, poverty, or unhappiness ... through the art and affirmations.

Faridi McFree

CELEBRATE YOU!

What Is Self-Healing Through Art?

Art healing deals with energy ... a combination of my energy and your energy!

Energy is a vibration ... and all color, line, form and affirmations create vibrations on their own specific wavelengths or frequencies.

Further, scientists are presently examining and studying the invisible vibrations that surround people. Kirlian photography, which has been able to capture these vibrations, has recorded different colored auras that surround us. Fear, anxiety, anger, worry, and hate (negative emotions) have been photographed and identified as LOW-FREQUENCY ENERGIES.

On the other hand, Love, Creativity, Optimism, Happiness (Positive Emotions) have been recorded as HIGH FREQUENCY ENERGIES ... and the higher frequency with which you surround yourself, the better you will feel. In other words, some energies weaken you, others strengthen you ... depending upon the vibrations.

Have you ever noticed that after being with a certain type of personality for a while you begin to feel drained? Yet, other people have the opposite effect ... their energy is so uplifting!

Allow the art on these pages to draw you into its vibration and begin to notice the magic of my energy mixed with yours. Not only will it be exciting and adventurous, but each day will be filled with all kinds of surprises. Lift your vibration to a higher frequency and move into higher levels of energy. Be happy, healthy, and prosperous!

My energy, which is healing, is transmitted through my art and affirmations and generates Positive Thoughts and Emotions:

It creates . . . Faith
Inspiration
Honesty
Sensitivity
Determination
Love
Peace
Happiness
Optimism
Charity
Confidence
Unselfishness
Goodness
Expectation
Courage
Compassion
Security
Enthusiasm
Vision
Ambition
Patience
Creativity
Goodwill . . .

and brings good luck and money, too!

What Is An Affirmation?

"Affirmations are statements of truth, which when spoken with conviction, are a strong vibratory force that destroys negative thoughts, wrongful habits, and harmful mental patterns which cause ill health, anxiety and fear. Affirmations, repeated continually with concentration, stimulate and direct the flow of life energy to bring about physical, mental and spiritual healing. . . ."

PARAMAHANSA YOGANANDA

Here Are Some Examples Of Affirmations:

"I AM GETTING BETTER EVERY DAY AT EVERYTHING THAT I DO AND SAY."

"I LOVE MYSELF UNCONDITIONALLY AND OTHERS TOO."

"I AM WORTHY OF LOVE AND HAPPINESS."

The art and affirmations will act as catalysts to help heal the emotions, and your own self-healing abilities will be developed and unblocked, enabling you to change your negative thought patterns and create positive action in your life. . . .

Art And Affirmations For ...

Reinforcement of Health
Improvement of Self-Image
Stress Reduction
Risking as Growth
Living Holistically Everyday
Emotional Growth Resulting in Love
Transcending Negative Patterns and Depression
Self-Respect
Development of Inner Authority
Self-Discipline
Releasing Unlimited Creative Potential
Releasing Emotional Distress
Increased Positive Energy
Releasing Negative Emotions

Eliminate the Negative Thoughts, Feelings, and Words. . . .

Fear
Hate
Anger
Worry
Resentment
Jealousy
Revenge
Selfishness
Greed
Envy
Pessimism
Frustration
Anxiety
Insecurity . . .

to release Positive Energy. . . .

Today, more and more, doctors and scientists are realizing that negative emotions destroy and positive emotions heal . . .

Depression can be described as magnified and inappropriate negative response to life experiences. It may surface in many forms. ...

Some examples are:

The reduction or total disappearance of enjoyment and pleasure, sleep problems, fatigue, loss of confidence, guilt, indecision, lack of caring about people or things, irritability and thoughts of suicide.

Also, physical disorders may manifest ... such as, nausea, headaches, chest pains, stomach cramps ... however, no organic cause for the complaints are ever found!

How To Accelerate A More Positive Self-Image Use Of Art And Affirmations

These highly positive affirmations are designed to help change your thinking . . . therefore, your situation in life.

Read this book at least two or three times during the day. Morning and night are especially important. While reading the art book, chant or sing the affirmations aloud. Meditate on the art and affirmations . . . whenever and how often you can. Write each affirmation at least twenty times a day. Invent new ways of using the book. The art has a magical way of making the creative process flow, so this should be easy.

Remember . . . it is natural to feel good about yourself!

Further in the book, you will find meditation and visualization exercises to instruct you to change your inner attitudes.

The art and affirmations
will help you change your
present limited concepts and
beliefs about yourself and
the world you live in.

Drop the barriers of your
negative expectations and
experience health, happiness,
love, creativity, peace of
mind, optimism, and joy.

I am a person of value

I will always think great thoughts

I am talented

I am the star of my own show

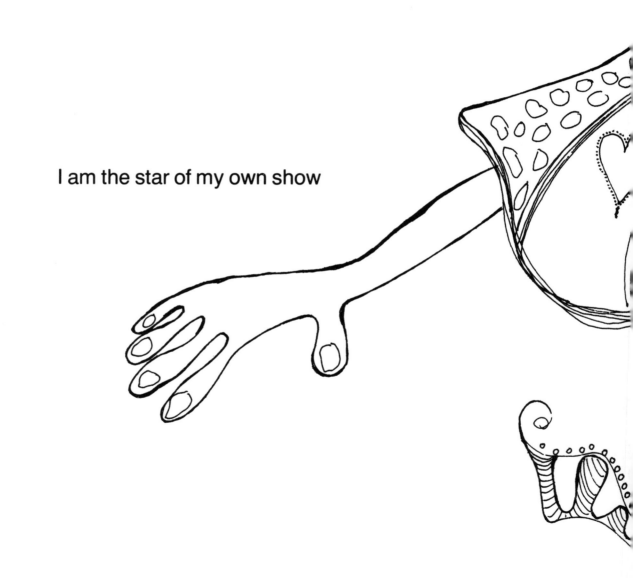

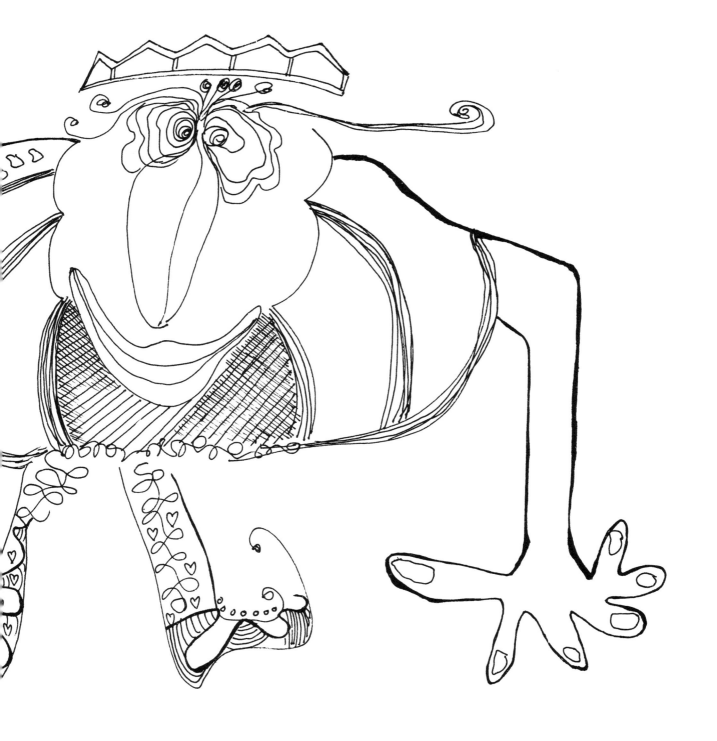

I always find
It starts in the mind
It all begins with you
What you visualize
Will materialize
To fit your point of view
So think the best
And watch the test
Of making your positive self-image come true . . .

I am determined to create a positive
world for myself

I am open to change

I am determined to see things differently

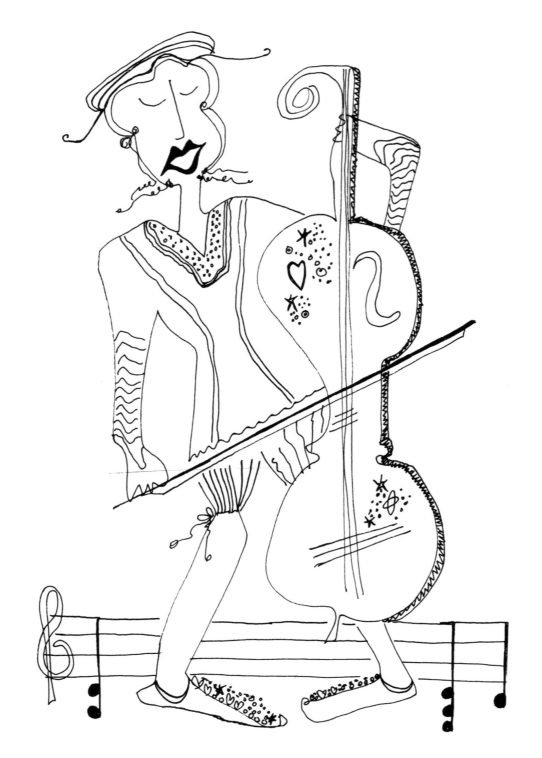

Meditation Exercise

Meditate on the affirmation of your choice for at least five minutes.

Think of the negative thoughts that prevent you from achieving success, (insecurity, fears, doubts, and jealousy).

Write down the affirmation at least twenty times. See yourself living the affirmation now.

Visualization Exercise

Close your eyes.

Take three deep breaths.

Sit in silence.

Repeat the affirmation of your choice several times. In the middle of your forehead, imagine balloons flowing out of you. See them in detail. Each balloon represents your fears and negative attitudes that prevent you from achieving success.

Release each negative attitude by means of a balloon.

In the center of your forehead, visualize yourself living your affirmation now.

Suggested listening, "healing music" to the above exercises: Mark Halpern's *"Spectrum Suite."*

I will live with the
spontaneity of a child

I am kind to myself
every day

I am healthy, strong, and vital

I appreciate my own uniqueness

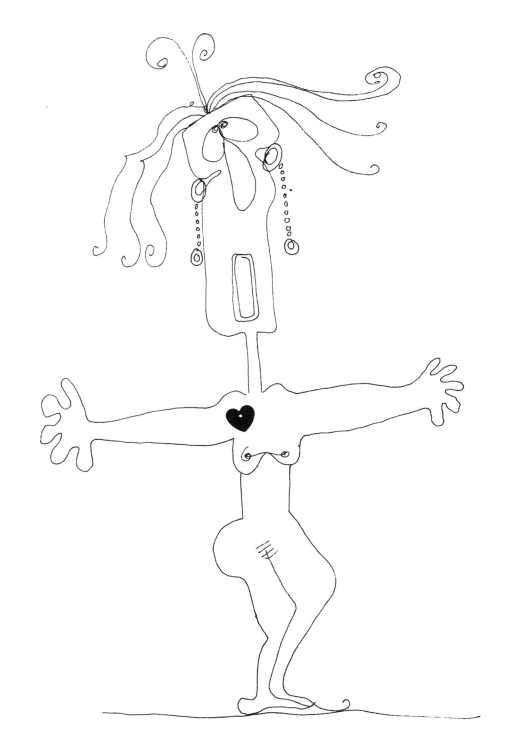

I am going to be myself today

i Realize my only enemies live in my negative thoughts and i have the power

to cleanse and heal my thinking.........

Be kind to Yourself
Sark

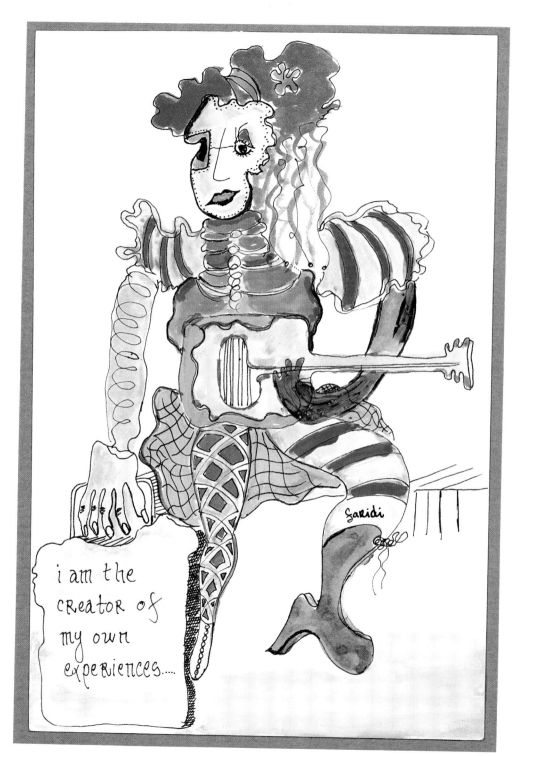

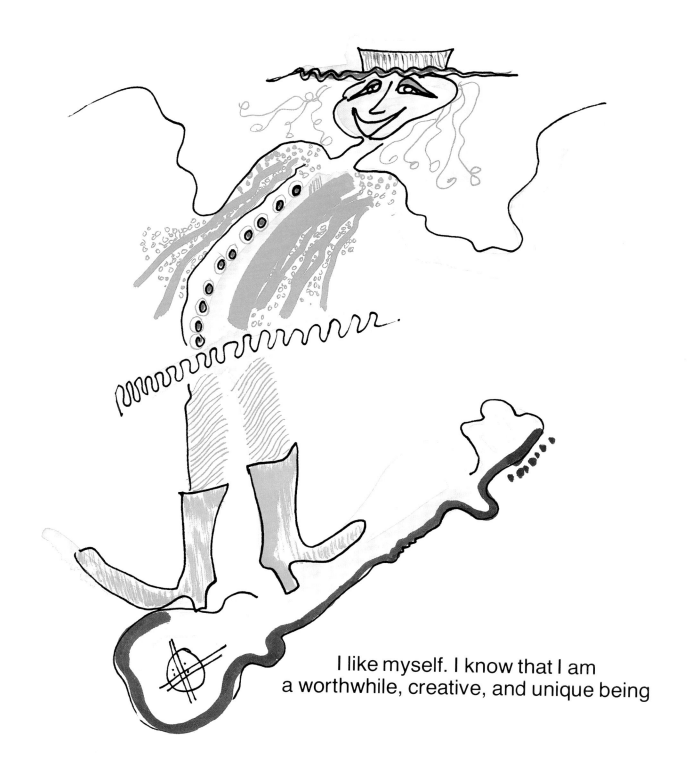

I like myself. I know that I am
a worthwhile, creative, and unique being

I don't have to rehearse
to be myself

I have unlimited potential

I improve with age

Not only do emotional disorders and problems affect individuals' joy of life and their families as well, but, according to FBI estimates, about twenty percent of police deaths and twenty-eight percent of assaults on police officers occur while officers are intervening in family fights. . . .

I will always strive to have positive
thoughts about myself and others

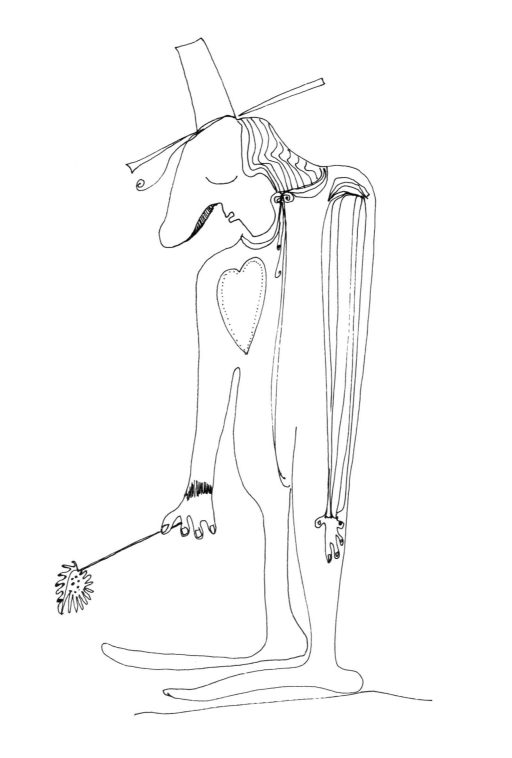

I am developing loving and
harmonious relationships
with others

I have a warm regard for others
at all times and in all situations

I accept my mistakes as evidence of change

Every day, in every way, I accomplish
more than I did the previous day

I easily overcome any obstacles

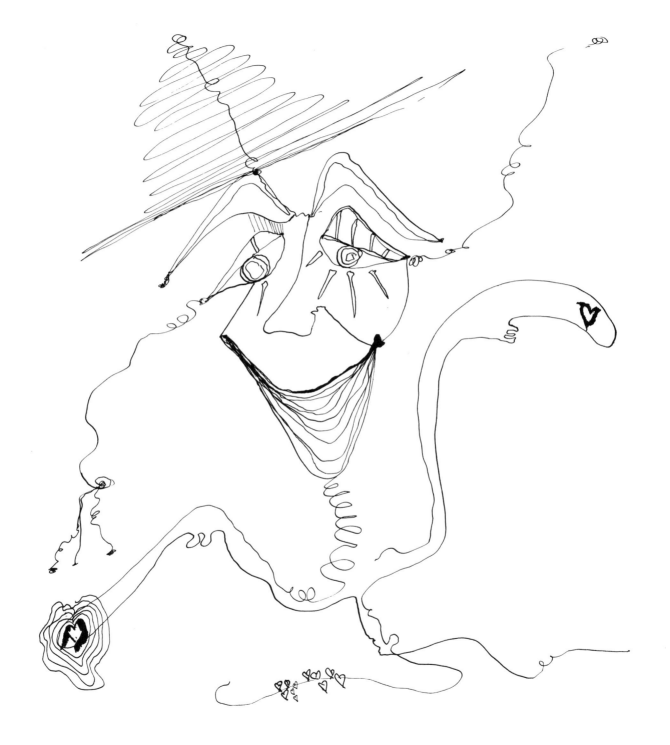

The past is over . . . it cannot hurt me anymore

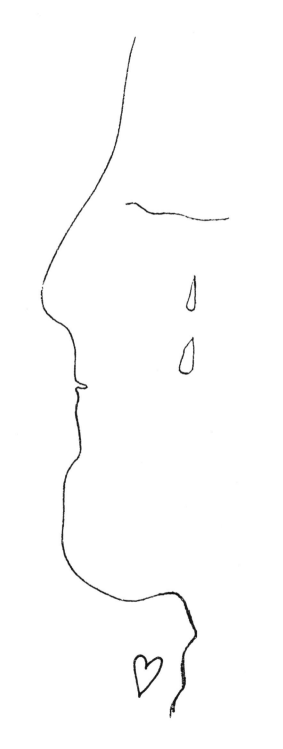

How Affirmed Are You?

Do you know what the negative emotions are that cause you and your family all kinds of trouble?

Which one do you have to work on?

Which ones do your children have to work on?

Which ones are you stuck in that are causing physical dis-ease?

We must recognize that negativism helps breed wars, starvation, mental and physical dis-ease, violence and catastrophes. . . .

How long will it take us
to feel good about ourselves
and others so that our children
can grow up in environments
fostering love, peace, optimism,
creativity, and goodwill towards
themselves and others?

About The Artist/Healer/Teacher/Performer

The stylized art of Faridi McFree depicts colorful figures who proclaim love, creativity, joy, optimism, success, and health. "We have been programmed for so many years to think negative thoughts about ourselves that we have lost sight of our true nature," says Faridi. "My art and affirmations help you to become yourself, whosoever that is . . . and you will become more and more centered."

No matter where you live, what your origin, color, country, social or financial station in life, you will feel good about being yourself . . . just being you. There are no boundaries to Faridi's affirmations and art . . . human or geographic.

Faridi, who has been compared to Picasso and Steinberg, studied at Parsons School of Design, New York School of Interior Design, Woodstock Artists Association, and the Art Students League in New York City. She also studied at the Art Center and UCLA in California.

A graduate of SILVA MIND CONTROL and ACTU-ALIZATIONS, Faridi developed her own techniques and puts them to good use in Art Performances and Workshops in Art Healing in Los Angeles and New York City. Her work has been recognized with radio and television interviews. Among the "new age" artists who have experienced her work with amazing results is LYNN SCHROEDER, co-author of "SUPERLEARNING" and "THE PSYCHIC EXPERIENCES BEHIND THE IRON CURTAIN." Faridi has performed at: THE ANANDA ASHRAM; BEVERLY HILLS HOLISTIC CENTER; THE FREEMAN INSTITUTE IN LOS ANGELES; THE BEACON THEATRE IN NEW YORK CITY FOR "CAMBODIAN CHILDREN/THE DAY OF THE CHILD"; MILTON J. GOODMAN LEAGUE OF POSTGRADUATE CENTER FOR MENTAL HEALTH/BILTMORE HOTEL IN NEW YORK CITY; THE HOLISTIC CENTER AT HAZEL HILLS FARM IN WISCONSIN; THE SALEM CHILDREN'S TRUST IN NEW HAMPSHIRE, A HOME FOR ABUSED, NEGLECTED, AND ABANDONED CHILDREN; EAST/WEST HOLISTIC CENTER, NEW YORK CITY.

Ms. McFree was married to Michael McFree for sixteen years. While they were married, Michael was a television agent at THE WILLIAM MORRIS AGENCY in New York City and also creative consultant to Merv Griffin in Los Angeles. During this period, Faridi was very inspired by the many interesting and unusual artists and celebrities she met and helped entertain with her husband. It was during this period that she was the art teacher for many artists' children, including Sara and Bob Dylan's five children.

An architectural designer, decorator, gourmet cook, free-spirited dancer, and presently studying acting and improvisational theater in New York City, Faridi believes there is no limitation to the mind.

She has also founded and developed FARIDI ENTERPRISES, UNLTD. . . . a company that develops greeting cards, stationery, publications, lithos, TV shows, video tape cassettes, and other "self-healing" products.

Inspirational Contributions

Jerry Siegel
Judy Freedman
Alan Freedman
The Bardey Family
The Gerngross Family
Robert Petro & Family
Jo Bernier & Family
Vincent Promuto
Bill Caspare
Parron Hopkins
Milton Hood Ward
George James
Jerry Belfert
Barbara Romo
Alan Mednick
Bart Andrews
John Macker
Susan Warren
Lynn Gordon
Lloyd Gaynes
Dr. & Mrs. Albert Freeman
Lena & Everett Freeman
Harold Tomin
Chicky Pullam III
Linda Hunter
Bob Stone
Raymond Marione
Mike Levine
Arnold Lewis
Jay Emmett
Dharani Bluestone & Friends
Linda Clark
Howard Graphics Designers
Marvin Ackerman & Friends
Aj Lagel
Nancy & John Magera
Dr. Walter Urban
Joe Cook

Jay Stevens
Joan & Hank Clark
The Binkiewicz Family
Gwenith Albucher
Barbara Contardi
William Hanft
David Zimmerman & Family
Elise Witlin
Lorraine & Elliott Lubin
Rose & Henry Frankel
Merrily & Bob Heck
Dr. Elan Neev
David Goldstein
Cy Schaffer
Dan Cirlin
Morty Roth
Gil Champion
Gayna Dunlap & Friends
Adele Khoury
Anita & Bob Logan & Girls
Ernie Patton
Curtis Dewey
Connie Mayer
Ron Laura
Barbara & Jay Speirs
Nancy Gabor
Grant Bishop
Stu Jackson
Janet & Leonard Kramer
Renee McCoy & Family
Linda & Ira Goldberg
David Goodman
Michelle Brourman & Family
Dr. Sage King & Family
Alan Rich & Family
Joan Dowd
Jim Avati & Family
Julieanne Thompson

Frank Clark
Ramona Wingate
Mrs. Aaron Bring
Helene Simich
Stephen Stewart
Carole Foster
Mary Coleman
Steve Hyman
Earl McGrew
Kara Blaum
Cary Nord
Carol Agate
Carol Belote, Bob & Girls
Murray Schwartz
Nat Lefkowitz
Merv Griffin
Sol Leon
John Rhinehart
Chris & Joel Martin
Sara Dylan & Children
Marvin Mitchelson
Kathy Hull
Lorraine Wohl
Lillian & Paul Tessler
Levon Helm & Family
Linda Lavin
Sally Struthers
Eileen Brennan
Jonathan Taplin
Joann McFree
June Graham
Jim Spencer
Bob Goldberg
The Obsatz Family
Larry Dumas
Cardinal Hayes Home
    For Children

Karen Gottlieb
Rosanna Soto
Joyce Chamberlain
Trish & Bob Pfeiffer
Lynn Schroeder
Dr. Ronee Hermann
Trent O. Meacham
Tamara Rand
Michael Pitkow
Rita Gusky
Liz Potter
David Zalaznick
Dr. Benjamin Weisman
Martin Wilens
Robert Chase
Jerry Schwartz
Jeff Becker
Frank Rosenberg
Arthur Weinthal & Family
Susanne Sommers
Al Hamil
Debbie & David Olson
Future Studios
Ron Williams
Jerome Metcalf & Friends
Aggie Ferguson
Stanley Hirsch
Basil Collier
Ruth & Steven Kriegsman
Tom Bunzel
Steve Zachary
Edgar Price
Diana & Bill Darrid
Elliot Shapiro
Ruben Preufs
Agnes & Gerri Berri
Salem Children Trust